Jodhpur . Jaisalmer

ISBN: 81-7436-396-3

© **Roli & Janssen BV 2005**
This edition published in 2005 in
arrangement with Roli & Janssen BV
The Netherlands
M-75 Greater Kailash II (Market)
New Delhi 110 048, India
Ph: ++91-11-29212782, 29210886
Fax: ++91-11-29217185
E-mail: roli@vsnl.com
Website: rolibooks.com

Editor: Priya Kapoor
Design: Arati Subramanyam
Layout: Naresh Mondal
Production: Naresh Nigam

Printed and bound in Singapore

Preceding page 1: *A fort wins its honours
in the desert not only from the battles it
survives, but also from the number of sati-
hand tablets it can boast; this tablet of 31
sati hands is from Mehrangarh's Loha Pol.*

This page: *Local musicians entertain
visitors at the pristine sand dunes of Sam,
near Jaisalmer.*

Following pages 4-5: *A caravan of camels:
this is how trade was once conducted across
the border and into the desert.*

Kishore Singh ❦ Karoki Lewis

Jodhpur Jaisalmer

❦

Lustre Press
Roli Books

Desert Kingdoms

Far out into the desert were two kingdoms ruled by princes who claimed their descent from the sun and the moon. Slowly they established their might over the desert and extended their sway, often coming into conflict with each other. In the isolation of their capitals, they remained in touch with world affairs, and made their outposts modern cities.

When Jodhpur was established over five centuries ago, its princes, not satisfied with what they held set off on missions of conquest. The foundation of Bikaner by Rao Bika became the most important historical offshoot, but other members of the family also established Idar, Kishengarg, Ratlam, Jhabua and Sailana. This happened, as Mahender Singh, former Yuvraj of Idar and great-grandson of the late Sir Pratap says, because 'those were very turbulent times in Indian history, exciting times.'

Indian princes witnessed turbulent times again in 1947 when their independent kingdoms were merged with the Indian union. On May 12, 1952, four-year-old Gaj Singh inherited the throne after his father's fatal air accident. Although Jodhpur had acceded to the Dominion of India in 1947, the young Gaj Singh was recognized the Maharaja of Jodhpur by Presidential decree, the thirty-eighth of his dynasty. Princely India finally ceased to exist in 1970, after Prime Minister Indira Gandhi abolished the royals' privy purses. The former maharajas found themselves selling family heirlooms for survival, converting their palatial residences into hotels.

The most impressive of these is Jodhpur's Umaid Bhawan; part hotel, part museum and residence for the royal family. The Jodhpur maharaja, Gaj Singh, has served as ambassador of India to Trinidad and Tobago, a Member of Parliament and actively involves himself in encouraging tourist interest in Jodhpur. The palace is but one example: the traditional Jodhpur seat is

Facing page:
Although their roles and powers have been reduced, the heads of ruling families still command respect and continue to celebrate festivals in the same traditional manner as their forefathers had once done. Here Maharawal Brijraj Singh of Jaisalmer is seen with former courtiers and nobles on his wedding day.

Following pages 8-9:
Maharaja Gaj Singh II of Jodhpur with his family. After the Indian government abolished privy purses for the princes Maharaja Gaj Singh II was one of the first to turn his heritage into an asset by converting his palace Umaid Bhawan, into a luxury hotel.

the fort of Mehrangarh and here Bapji, as he is fondly referred to, has created a magnificent museum. You can occasionally come across him in the palace; retainers bow low as he walks past; in his chambers, they do not disturb him but for the most important matters; his secretary hands him the telephone as if it were a fragile piece of china. Today his small close-knit family made up by his mother, wife and two children is involved in various conservation and development projects.

Rumour has it that Bapji's father, the last maharaja of Jodhpur, was killed on account of the popular vote bank he commanded: elections were round the corner. Whether this is true will probably never be known, but the royals, as history proves, always commanded passionate loyalty or hatred, the touchstones to kingdom-building in the desert.

That is probably what kept Jaisalmer going. This desert kingdom was truly cut off, yet a wonderful city from trading riches grew here, and Jaisalmer remained important till the sea-trade routes were started. Today, the Rajmata, the queen-mother, is in residence at the palace. She exchanged one isolated kingdom for another when she married, leaving the valley of Kathmandu for the sandy wastes of Jaisalmer while still a teenager. News from the outside world comes in the form of magazines and visits to Delhi; other than that, like Jaisalmer itself, the royal family lives in the present but has a very strong foundation in the past.

Introduction

The desert has been there for millenia, a sea of tawny gold, crested silver by moonlight, scorching in noonday summer. Petrified forest fossils and those of crustaceans, sea shells and minerals lend promise to the claim that the Thar was not always barren waste. If there was once water here, it is extremely rare and very precious now. What geological shift in the plates of the earth caused the ocean to dry up? We do not yet know. But in India, scientific facts often lose their relevance anyway, and there is mention in the great epics of the sea. According to at least one interpretation, when Lord Ram was made to cross the ocean to the island of Lanka where Ravana had his golden capital to rescue his wife, Sita, the Lord of the Sea turned him back. The incensed Ram fitted to his bow an arrow of such immense destructive potential that the Lord of the Sea retreated, assigning him permission to make the crossing. Alas, the arrow, once mounted, could not be recalled. Ram then shot the arrow in another direction, aimed at a sea of water, and such was the heat it generated that the vast body of water dried up, and for more time than mankind can recall, there was no life here…

Fables are but a figment of the mind, but the sands shift and ripple in little waves, in memory of the ocean bed they once formed. During storms the whip of burning hot sand lashes, lacerates. Like ships lost at sea, caravans of camels have been known to disappear, never to be found again. Marusthali, the Region of Death, is a cruel place. The summers sizzle: all moisture is sapped from the air, every

Preceding pages 10-11: As Jaisalmer grew, people established homes outside its fortifications, but once the entire community used to live within the 12th-century fort established by the Bhatti descendants of Lord Krishna.

Facing page: Desert women wear dazzling colours and veil their faces, a tradition that is believed to have begun with the Muslim invasion of India.

living thing scorched, bleached, drained. Years go by without rain; in winter, it is freezing cold. This is scrub desert, with little vegetation. What little grows that is edible is dried and stored, to be eaten through the year.

What people, then, made the desert their home? Who gave it its fragile, fairytale palaces and mansions? What made them stay, what imperative directed them to brave the harsh desert, conquering it with their spirit, habiting it with ritual and imperial significance, waging mighty battles for a land so forlorn? And what promise brought foreign invaders to this land, with what hopes, to what gain?

The Rajputs are fire-born, a martial race tracing their lineage to the sun-god (and in some cases the moon god). Called Suryavanshis —sun-descended—or Chandravanshis—moon-descended—this great race, that once held all of what was loosely known as Hindustan under its sway, believes the great Lord Ram to be an

Religious and secular wall paintings adorn walls of desert homes; these paintings were made to celebrate a wedding in the family.

ancestor. The Rajputs themselves branched off into different families; internecine battles, and the continuing onslaught of foreign invaders, found their power structure being eroded. Chased out of their seat of power in the medieval ages, they travelled over the country seeking not refuge—that would have been alien to their spirit—but sovereignty. Their quest for their own fiefdoms brought them in turn to what is contemporary Rajasthan.

This alien land proved their final settling ground. A strong lure was the desert trade routes over which they could exercise their control. Caravans from distant Egypt and Afghanistan passed through the desert. The Rajput chieftains levied a tax on their passage and in turn offered them safe custody through their kingdoms, protection against the earlier local tribal chieftains, who would loot at will. The traders were more than happy to pay for this concession, and it was on the proceeds of these that the princely

The entrance to a house is painted with the auspicious Ganesh, and cattle wander casually past.

kingdoms thrived. In times to come, allegiance with the Mughal court in Agra and Delhi, and with Calcutta under the British, provided additional revenues in the nature of grants, and as the wages of loyalty.

The destruction of court records of the Rajputs' early history and the search for new kingdoms left little by way of historical documents and written evidence. Certain feats of valour were eulogized by the court poets attached to the rulers. The earliest definitive chronicle of the Rajputs was written by Colonel James Tod in the early 19th century as the *Annals and Antiquities of Rajasthan* and they still provide the most comprehensive history of its tribes and rulers. Colonel Tod was struck by the similarities between the Rajputs and certain western warrior races, and it may be relevant here to quote some of his observations:

> Ku-mara is the Rajput god of war. He is represented with seven heads in the Hindu mythology: the Saxon god of war has six.
>
> The religion of the martial Rajput, and the rites of Har, the god of battle, are little analogous to those of the meek Hindus, the followers of the pastoral divinity, the

This page: Not only are the women of Rajasthan beautiful, they also wear jewellery literally from head to toe. Most popular among the ornaments worn in the desert are the rakhri, worn on the temple, and the chura, graded ivory bangles sported by all married women.

Facing page: Around Jodhpur are a number of Bishnoi settlements. Bishnoi women such as these, dress very colourfully; their men, in contrast, wear stark white.

worshippers of kine, and feeders on fruits, herbs, and water. The Rajput delights in blood: his offerings to the god of battle are sanguinary, blood and wine. The cup (*cupra*) of libation is the human skull. He loves them because they are emblematic of the deity he worships; and he is taught to believe that Har loves them, who in war is represented with the skull to drink the foeman's blood, and in peace is the patron of wine and women. With Parbutti on his knee, his eyes rolling from the juice of the p'fool and opium, such is this Bacchanalian deity of war. Is this Hinduism, acquired on the burning plains of India? Is it not rather a perfect picture of the manners of the Scandinavian heroes?

The Rajput slays buffaloes, hunts and eats the boar and deer, and shoots ducks and wild fowl; he worships his horse, his sword, and the sun, and attends more to the martial song of the bard than to the litany of the Brahmin. In the martial mythology and warlike poetry of the Scandinavians a wide field exists for assimilation, and a comparision of the poetical remains of the Asi of the east and west would alone suffice to suggest a common origin.

Preceding pages 18-19: Women of the Rajasthan desert wear bright colours and lots of jewellery, unlike the inhabitants of most other deserts, where the colours are soft and blend with the environment. These are Banjara gypsy performers in Jaisalmer.

This page and left: The different styles of tying a turban distinguish the various tribes found amongst the people of the desert.

21

Some of the finest stone carving in the desert are seen on the window balconies of Jaisalmer, the work of both Hindu and Muslim craftsmen.

Facing page: Havelis are the pride of Jaisalmer architecture. Here a busy lane in front of Patwon Ki Haveli, a group of five mansions owned by brocade merchants who started the grand havelis building tradition in Jaisalmer.

Colonel Tod listed in his treatise a catalogue of 36 royal races in Rajasthan, and attempted to trace their genealogy. Of these, only two have relevance for the purpose of this book—the Rathore clan that ruled over Jodhpur, and the Bhatti clan of Jaisalmer. The Rathores were enthroned at Kanauj in the 5th century. The Chauhans ruled from Delhi, and when due to internal strife Delhi fell, Kanauj followed 'and while its last prince, Jaichand, found a grave in the Ganges, his son sought asylum in Marusthali, the Region of Death. Seoji was this son; the founder of the Rathore dynasty in Marwar, on the ruins of the Pariharas of Mandore. Here they brought their ancient martial spirit…' and over generations, finding Mandore exposed, shifted their capital to Jodhpur, named after its founder, Rao Jodha.

As for the Bhattis of Jaisalmer, their lineage is no less impressive, for these are lunar-descended Rajputs who look to Krishna as the head of their race. According to Tod, the Yadu or Yadava race was driven out of Delhi and Dwarka following the death of Krishna, but his sons passed the Indus and peopled the reaches upto Samarkhand. After some time they were driven out of these countries 'whether it was owing to the Greek princes who ruled all these countries for a century after Alexander, or to the rise of Islamism', and in India too their occupation of the Punjab was challenged till they found themselves driven to the desert where, defeating the local tribes, they occupied Lodurva and then shifted and established in the early 12th century the kingdom of Jaisalmer named after its founder, Raja Jaisal.

Having exhausted their power in other parts of India, the Rajputs peopled the tracts of the desert and gave it a life that no other desert in the world can claim. Staunch forts stand sentinel in the desert, within them delicate palaces and apartments; colours run riot, in the sussuration of skirts and the fold of turbans; religion is a living philosophy, and the tradition has bequeathed a number of temples and house-deities; splendid jewels, hierarchy, courts and the ceremony of kinship are keenly observed.

History is proof that the vintage of cities in the desert is so recent as to be nascent. Named after their founders, the two cities

The tractor is a recent introduction to the desert, for agriculture is largely dependent on the rainfall, which proves elusive, year after year. The tractor is nevertheless put to good use, often as a means of transport for families.

that were once mighty, independent kingdoms were Jaisalmer and Jodhpur; the first of these, the stronghold of the Bhatti Rajputs, is truly a gilded city close to the Indian border with Pakistan. Jaisalmer was founded in the 12th century; Jodhpur is just over five hundred years old. Jodhpur had shifted to its impregnable fortified location from nearby Mandore, and Jaisalmer from Lodurva.

The early years of each settlement were spent as much in consolidation as in aggressive expansion. The local chiefs paid their obeisance before the warlords, were offered protection and positions of power and honour in court. Certain privileges were granted to them; revenue collection, for instance, or the anointing of the new king. The kingdoms were strange—fortified capitals, and for miles around a desolate landscape with few villages, fewer people. Yet, having set their roots, built their forts, and banded together armies of loyal followers, the desert kings put up a resistance to any claim on their land by invading armies. They fought to a man, and often died to a man. To dull the sensation of pain in war, their armies often dressed in saffron and opiated their senses, fighting to the proverbial last breath. Their women would, on such occasions, commit *jauhar*, a ritual of self-immolation in flaming pits of fire, for what daughter of the sun-god would be held captive in the harems of invaders? Often, women in their hundreds, if not in their thousands, performed this ritual, the head-ranis leaving behind their handprints on the walls of the fort. Forts that have waged war, and seen this sacrifice by their womenfolk, are held in high esteem in Rajasthan, and the desert forts have their own share of these valorous deeds to tell. The most poignant of these describes the ritual of *jauhar* when the citadel of Jaisalmer was stormed in the 13th century and 24,000 women and children embraced death

Tourism has brought with it a new religion of international tolerance and understanding— and a new cuisine that is western by residents' standards and incomprehensible to tourists. The language on the billboards may be funny, but clearly tourism has revamped the economy in Jaisalmer!

rather than captivity. It was also in Jaisalmer, when invaded, that a ruler himself went about the task of beheading his wives and concubines, for there was little time left for performing *jauhar*, and the siege laid by the invaders was strong; yet, Jaisalmer won the field, and the royal women lost their lives in vain.

Desert architecture is characterized by two distinctive traits, fortification and the need to provide sanctuary from the heat. Invasions were rarely, if ever, mounted in the hot summer months; the acute shortage of water, and the shimmering desert haze, with its mirages, dissuaded the most valorous from waging offensives. But this was a time for erecting fortifications, and finding means of more

25

Built by 3,000 workers over a 15-year period, Jodhpur's Umaid Bhawan is currently a hotel and the royal residence.

Preceding pages 26-27: *Jaisalmer's rich architectural legacy is represented here in the Patwon Ki Haveli. The wealthy traders of Jaisalmer could afford the finest available talent due to their control over the trade routes. These havelis are built in such a way as to allow breeze even at the hottest point of the day.*

elaborate protection. Fortifications tended to merge with the lay of the land. If the fort at Jaisalmer has battlements that reflect the rounded curves of the dunes that surround it, the hilltop Mehrangarh at Jodhpur rises such that the fort walls and sheer basalt escarpment are indistinguishable one from the other. Huge gates guarded entry to the forts, usually spiked with iron nails so that elephants could not be used to bring these down. From the battlements, vents were provided for pouring hot oil on those attempting to scale the walls. Unlike Mughal forts, those of the Hindu desert kings were a labyrinthine maze of warrens and corridors, all narrow, reached by staircases that too were small; it was easier to defend these: even one person could hold back a posse of soldiers as women and children made good their escape.

The royal apartments within the fort, and the havelis of the rich merchants, were more delicately designed. They were usually high, to allow in any hint of air; often they were shielded by stone screens that, while providing protection from the unrelenting vigil of the sun, also broke the pattern of the faintest wafts of air into cooling curtains of breeze. Certainly the interiors were splendid, for the Rajputs were aesthetic, and had the walls painted with a filigree of motifs in a rich mosaic of colours. There were windows set with stained glass so that the light shone through brilliantly; master painters executed breathtakingly beautiful miniatures; visiting artists were extended courtesies and patronage. In memory of often truant rains, there was usually a Badal Mahal or Palace of the Clouds, painted in the pleasing blue colours of sky and rain. Invariably, there would be a Sheesh Mahal, a motif the desert kings borrowed from the more powerful *gaddi* of Delhi and Agra; little mirrors set into ceilings and walls, shimmering brightly in the light of oil lamps, reflecting the flicker of the flame in a million images. Screened corridors were set aside for the royal women of the harem who observed purdah, and they often sat behind similar screens in halls overlooking a courtyard where a nautch dance might be in progress, or revels of some form being celebrated.

The kings kept elephants, a few of them, to reflect their pomp. The camel, ubiquitous here, was not used for royal journeys, but often in battle. The sun god had his chariot of twenty-four horses, housed in the royal stables. The number of horses constituted an important component of an army, and later the Mughal emperors often won the Rajputs' favour with generous gifts of foot soldiers and horses. The desert does not breed horses locally, and the finest of the species had often to be imported from Afghanistan and other regions of Asia. Good horsemen, the Rajputs later adopted the game of polo as their royal preserve, playing polo *chukkars* with skill and tenacity.

Shikar was another royal privilege. The winter months in the desert provide a wide variety of wildlife, wild boar, deer and partridge and that

Stone was treated like timber in Jaisalmer, where it was carved into window screens to allow privacy for women and serve a cooling purpose.

delectable game bird, the imperial sand grouse, a winter visitor migrating to these tracts from Siberia. The royals perfected the art of shikar and later used it as one of their most artful forms of diplomacy. The Jodhpurs perfected the art of pig-sticking, for there was wild boar to be found in good numbers in the stony tracts around the capital. Jodhpur's crusty Sir Pratap Singh has become something of a legend for his doings as regent and advisor to the throne. It is said that Edward VII, then Prince of Wales, once went pig-sticking at Jodhpur, but refused to stay mounted on his steed. Sir Pratap rode up to him and acidly remarked in his somewhat imperfect English: 'I know you Prince of Wales; you know you Prince of Wales; but *pig* no know you Prince of Wales'. Clearly unused to being spoken to in this manner, the Prince of Wales climbed back on his horse and the expedition continued, but how many pigs he eventually bagged is not known.

Yet in this very land, where shikar was a hobby of the nobles, live the Bishnois, a community of nature's conservationists. Drive out of Jodhpur, and you will pass Bishnoi settlements, the area recognizable by its greener surroundings and, often, the presence of deer roaming so carelessly as to be tame. It is said that a sage, Guru Jambeshwar, asked them to provide protection to all living things, even at the risk of their own lives. The Bishnois are vegetarians who do not allow the felling of trees or the killing of birds and animals, and if you come as friends, will greet you in a rather unorthodox fashion, with opium cupped in their palms. The men always dress in white, only their turbans flamboyant both in colour and the method of draping. The women wear bold earth colours and large quantities of silver jewellery.

Although their settlements were new, the desert kings were of ancient lineage, accustomed to the splendour of court. Thus it was that patronage was extended to artisans and craftsmen, and the desert became one of the richest repositories of the arts. Unlike in other deserts, such as the Gobi or the Sahara, where

the people invariably clothe themselves in white, the residents of the Thar wear brilliant colours—red, yellow, pink, green—shot with threads of gold, immense quantities of silver and gold jewellery. Women drape themselves in mantles that have been tie-dyed in a bright mosaic of colours, each pattern and colour with its own significance. A woman who produces an heir for the family claims the privilege of the *peeliya,* a dress in yellow with red motifs; while the daughter of a house may face male members of the family with equanimity, the daughter-in-law must hide her face from their gaze.

In their seclusion, the women sought refuge in the arts, and in beautifying themselves. Their surroundings were made lovelier with court artists commissioned to paint every blank piece of wall, ceiling, pillar and arch. Fabrics were specially hand-printed; family jewellers worked ceaselessly to keep them in newer, more exotic jewels; cobblers worked to encase their feet in silver slippers

Women carrying water from a well; these are everyday hardships, borne with great fortitude.

Following pages 32-33:
A view of the imperial city of Jodhpur from Mehrangarh. Umaid Bhawan is visible on the far right.

31

The women of Rajasthan wear jewellery as a complete ensemble and not just as an accessory.

embroidered with coloured threads and beads. The desert craftsmen proved able architects, sculptors, carpenters, and no item of utility was too small to escape their attentions. Camel hide was painted with gold to make small phials for storing the precious *asha*, a liqueur that was constituted of distilled saffron or rose and embellished with such aphrodisiacal components as crushed pearls and ground gold, with chunks of goat and sheep brains left to impart it a distinctive quality over years in storage.

Desert cuisine was often one of making-do. A peasant meal in the state is not particularly memorable, but the royal kitchens did have a rudimentary gourmet quality to them. There was little availability of fresh vegetables or pulses. The Rajput kitchen therefore became a specialist of sorts in dry meat preparations, venison and rabbit being particular favourites. This often meant shikar. If a rabbit was available, desert hare actually, it was skinned and cleaned, stuffed with spices and herbs, and buried in a sand pit under a layer of coal embers that were kept alive till the cooked rabbit was removed and served whole. More often, the chieftains dined on *sule*, venison or lamb marinated in *kachri* powder and barbecued. More modest fare was vegetarian, often composed of gram flour cubes in a hot gravy, the local dried vegetables of *sangri* and *gwarphali*, eaten with thick unleavened bread called *bajra*.

The Rajputs brought with them song and dance to the desert. The voice of the desert singers is deep and powerful, and their unusual string instruments carry a haunting melody. These instruments can be seen at Jodhpur's Mehrangarh Fort where they are housed in a museum, but the music is best experienced in Jaisalmer. Here, on a full moon night balladeers sit on dune crests and play their melody, give voice to their song—a powerful experience for the visitor.

The desert is also home to several folk dance forms. Members of different communities have their own distinctive

dances, and among these one of the most mesmerizing is the *tera talli* dance, in which women are seated cross-legged; as they sway from side to side, they clash cymbals, and gradually add to the repertoire as the beat picks up momentum, balancing a number of terracotta pots on their head and placing in their mouths a naked sword. The *sapera* dance by members of the snake-charmer community is electrifying. The Rajputs have no public performances. Their women dance the *ghoomar* within their homes on festive occasions.

The Aravalli hills run across the state, and literally denote their name: a beam lying across. This beam divides the more fertile tracts of Rajasthan from its western dry landscape. This is the desert, the domain of the hardiest Rajput kingdoms, indomitable bastions to two of its princely kingdoms, the desert cities of Jodhpur and Jaisalmer.

Music and dance are very much part of the eternal appeal of this wondrous land. There is a tradition of popular poetry and story telling through music.

Following pages 36-37:
Within the desert the camel is still the best and sometimes the only means of transportation. Justly called the ship of the desert, it can go for days without water, and its hooves are particularly well suited to traverse the soft, sinking sand.

Jodhpur

When the Rathore Rajputs ceased to be a power in Kanauj and were driven out, the 'wreck of their vassalage' travelled in search of a kingdom of their own. These sun-descended rulers made Marusthali, 'Region of Death', their home. Trade routes gave them much of their revenues, but because the desert yielded no obvious gain, several Rathore generations fortified themselves till they were finally seen as a challenge to the might of the empire in Delhi, then ruled by the Afghan usurper, Sher Shah Suri. When the Rathores clashed with Sher Shah, the emperor was led to exclaim that he 'had nearly lost the crown of India for a handful of barley'—an allusion to the barrenness of the desert.

Jodhpur was founded in 1459 when Rao Jodha, on the dictates of a hermit, moved his capital from Mandore to an impregnable hilltop. This was Mehrangarh, an eyrie that rose from the sharp cliffs, almost indistinguishable from them. Rao Jodha chose this place as his capital because of its strategic location on the edge of the Thar desert. Eight successive gates (there are now only seven) controlled entry to this fortified settlement and offered it protection. From the ramparts of Mehrangarh that span some ten kilometres, and are wide and spacious for sentry watch, one can look down upon the city with its many whitewashed homes. There is the occasional temple tower or residence of an aristocrat that breaks through the white-blue scramble of houses, and to one side Chattar Hill catches the eye. Atop this slight incline is another handsome building. This is Umaid Bhawan, believed to be the

Facing page:
The hill-fort bastions of Mehrangarh overlook a mushrooming town with its blinding white houses; on a clear day one can spot Kumbalgarh, another hill-fort some eighty miles away.

Following pages 40-41:
Maharaja Gaj Singh II with his family in formal attire against the backdrop of Umaid Bhawan, the formidable palace built as one of the largest personal residences in the world.

MAHARAJA TAKHT SINGH, 1843.

MAHARAJA JASWANT SINGH II, G.C.S.I. 1873.

MAHARAJA SARDAR SINGH, SUCCEEDED IN 1895.

largest personal residence in the world. Its chief architect, H.V. Lancaster, was not particularly imaginative; his buildings carry the stamp of solidity and state architecture. He would have liked a chance at building the British capital in Delhi, and chafed that the honour should have gone instead to Sir Edward Lutyens. The palace in Jodhpur was a chance to prove his credentials, and he set out to eclipse the Viceregal Lodge (now the Rashtrapati Bhawan) in New Delhi.

Umaid Bhawan is a perfectly symmetrical, formal building. Its 347 rooms employ few devices of local Rajput architecture, one of the few concessions being the circular ring of corridors with their screens, behind which the purdah women walked in privacy. The palace had its several courtyards, some for the exclusive use of the zenana women. Among its features were the first lifts and airconditioning systems introduced in Indian palaces, and, of course, electricity. The site of Chattar Hill was auspiciously ordained, but proved an inopportune one for its builders. It had no water; earth had to be carried on donkeys from the base of the hill so that it could be evened out for the construction of the large palace and its gardens, and a special railway line had to be laid over ten kilometres so that the sandstone with which it was built could be transported from the quarries.

Work on the palace began in 1929, a work force of over 3,000 laboured 15 years over its construction, and it was completed in 1945. Building work on the palace begun as a famine relief exercise when the monsoon failed for the third year running.

The palace had magnificent suites, the principal ones with the works of J.S Norblin, a Polish mural artist, and long baths carved out of a single block of black marble. At the centre of the palace were twin domes, the higher of which rose a hundred and ninety feet high, below it a whispering gallery. The palace had its own auditorium, a ballroom, a banquet hall for 300, eight more modest dining rooms, several kitchens, an underground swimming pool and doors of brass carved with the family insignia. For a desert palace it was cold and enclosing, not outward-looking as Rajput palaces are. But it was coloured and brought to life by

The insignia of the Jodhpur royal family inscribed on the gate of Umaid Bhawan.

Facing page:
A dynastic portrait of the rulers of Jodhpur. The Rathores claim descent from the sun and are said to have been created from the backbone of Lord Indra.

Following pages 44-45:
The interiors of Umaid Bhawan are reminiscent of the art nouveau tradition that flourished in the 1930s. The palace is now part royal residence, part museum and part luxury hotel.

Maharaja Gaj Singh II plays Holi, the festival of colours, with former courtiers and nobles.

Facing page:
Royal ancestry—the current maharaja of Jodhpur, Gaj Singh II, and his maharani pose for a formal picture in their living chambers at Umaid Bhawan.

the royal family, their traditions and rituals. Much of the palace's 1930s furniture was put together by local carpenters. The ship carrying the furniture from London originally intended for the palace was lost at sea. It was re-ordered, but the factory burnt down.

Today the palace, which retains its original magnificence, serves a number of functions. The Maharaja, fondly known as Bapji, occupies part of it and visitors can chance upon him in its many corridors or halls. His part of the building still has some of the finest princely possessions on display. Another part of the palace is a museum—a well-catalogued collection of mostly royal memorabilia, and a fascinating collection of clocks. The largest part of the palace is now a hotel, so it is possible to actually stay there, and be looked after by retainers who once waited on the royals.

Back along the winding road is Mehrangarh which was the traditional seat of governance, and where the act of coronation was

Mehrangarh built in the 15th century; in the foreground is Jaswant Thara, the memorial built in 1899 for Jodhpur's Maharaja Jaswant Singh.

till recently performed. A number of the apartments at Mehrangarh have had to be closed, but enough is open and on display for visitors to see for themselves the pageantry and ritual that was part of the royal lifestyle. Period rooms of the fort have been converted into a unique museum that houses a collection of palanquins, elephant howdahs, cradles, miniature paintings, weapons and turbans. It is now perhaps the best-preserved and maintained fort in Rajasthan.

Of great attraction is the Sileh Khana, the armoury with its dazzling display of swords, spears and daggers. Elsewhere, there is the throne of Jodhpur, a squat *gaddi* of gold, with its canopy richly embroidered with silver and gold threads and encrusted with gems. There are large numbers of palanquins, the sedan chairs on which the royals were carried in appropriate style and accompanied by musicians and armed guards. There are silver cradles and swings where children and young women once sat, and a richly assembled battle tent that belonged to Maharaja Abhai Singh—what war campaigns must have been planned under its canopy, what secrets shared or traded, what hopes and fears stifled? One of the most remarkable aspects of the fort is the collection and display of desert musical instruments, properly catalogued; some are still in use by wandering minstrels; others have fallen into disuse, and even professional musicians do not know how to play these. And there are the splendid halls, Durbar Mahal, Phool Mahal and Moti Mahal, rich with paintings, and windows with a delicate tracery of stone screens. A temple within the fort houses the royal family deity, to which members of the erstwhile ruling family still pay obeisance, attending ceremonies here on important occasions.

The Mehrangarh Fort Museum encompasses a series of palaces and houses a magnificent collection of memorabilia which reveals the heritage of the Rathores of Marwar. A superb audio tour in several international languages is available to accompany visitors through the Mehrangarh Fort and Museum.

The entrance from Loha Pol is marked by handprints (31 on one side and five on the other) of royal satis, the wives of maharajas. It is said that six queens and 58 concubines became satis on Ajit Singh's funeral in 1724. Jodhpur's chequered history provided its queens

The Glories of Mehrangarh

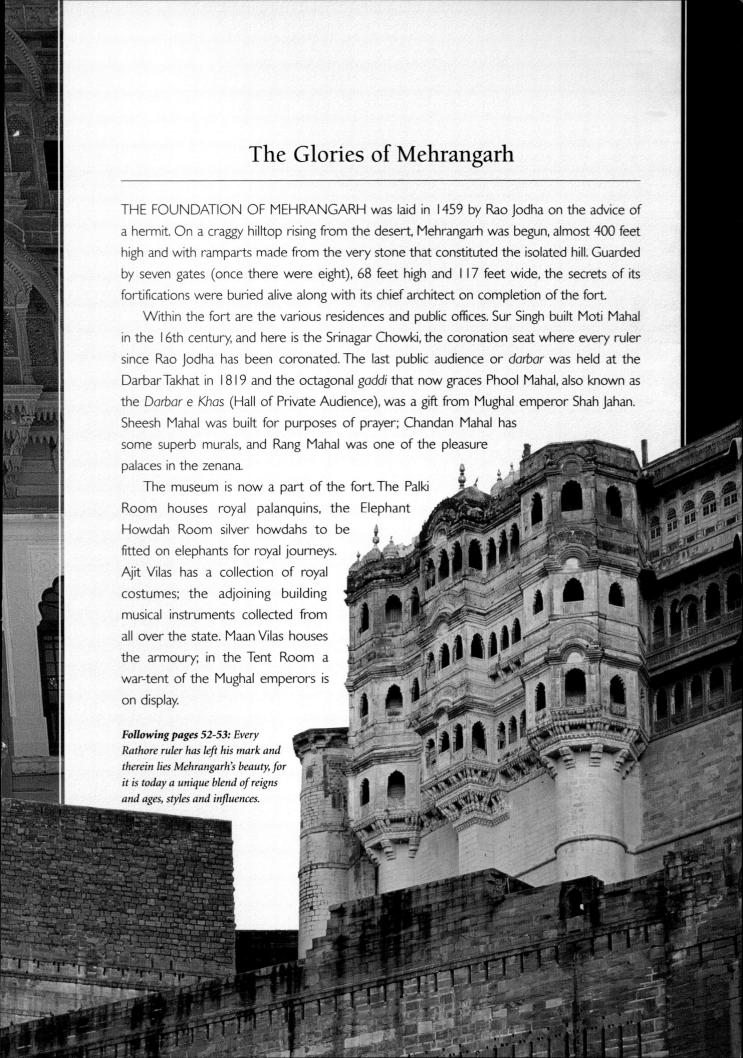

THE FOUNDATION OF MEHRANGARH was laid in 1459 by Rao Jodha on the advice of a hermit. On a craggy hilltop rising from the desert, Mehrangarh was begun, almost 400 feet high and with ramparts made from the very stone that constituted the isolated hill. Guarded by seven gates (once there were eight), 68 feet high and 117 feet wide, the secrets of its fortifications were buried alive along with its chief architect on completion of the fort.

Within the fort are the various residences and public offices. Sur Singh built Moti Mahal in the 16th century, and here is the Srinagar Chowki, the coronation seat where every ruler since Rao Jodha has been coronated. The last public audience or *darbar* was held at the Darbar Takhat in 1819 and the octagonal *gaddi* that now graces Phool Mahal, also known as the *Darbar e Khas* (Hall of Private Audience), was a gift from Mughal emperor Shah Jahan. Sheesh Mahal was built for purposes of prayer; Chandan Mahal has some superb murals, and Rang Mahal was one of the pleasure palaces in the zenana.

The museum is now a part of the fort. The Palki Room houses royal palanquins, the Elephant Howdah Room silver howdahs to be fitted on elephants for royal journeys. Ajit Vilas has a collection of royal costumes; the adjoining building musical instruments collected from all over the state. Maan Vilas houses the armoury; in the Tent Room a war-tent of the Mughal emperors is on display.

Following pages 52-53: Every Rathore ruler has left his mark and therein lies Mehrangarh's beauty, for it is today a unique blend of reigns and ages, styles and influences.

with several occasions to prove their fidelity to their lords. During Emperor Akbar's reign, Jodhpur princesses married the Mughal monarchs, and a time of relative peace came to pass. But following his death, a war of conflict broke out amongst his four sons, and Jodhpur backed the wrong prince; it was Aurangzeb who mounted the throne, and he was not easy to placate. Maratha and then British dominion stemmed all further growth till the late 19th century.

Much of Jodhpur's resurgence happened, under the personality of thrice-regent Sir Pratap Singh, who was described as 'a keen soldier, a lover of horse and hound, the intimate friend of three British sovereigns…' A loyalist, he was quite horrified when in 1885, journeying to London to meet the Queen, he lost his wardrobe *en route,* thus having to appear before her in less than his usual finery. Very pucca, he found French fashion and life decadent, and was sufficiently taken aback by one woman's *dècolletage* to remark to his companion: 'I think not very gentlemanly lady!'

This picture is from Jodhpur's Ajit Bhawan, where members of the former royal family have created a theme hotel.

Facing page: A royal wedding is characterized by pomp and splendour. Maharawal Brijraj Singh of Jaisalmer with his bride on his wedding day.

Following pages 56-57: On ceremonial occasions, the maharaja still returns to Mehrangarh, to be seated under the royal canopy and participate in durbars.

Jodhpur's streets are delightfully awash with colour. The trousseaus of most Rajput girls are tailored and embroidered in Jodhpur, and orders are specially catered to, for the wedding dress cannot simply be picked up from a shop. Jodhpur is also well known for having given the world *jodhpurs,* riding breeches that are baggy till the knee and then fit tight along the rest of the leg, to be worn under riding boots. In fact it is Sir Pratap who is credited with inventing the now famous jodhpurs. Around 1890 Sir Pratap started wearing riding breeches tailored for the game. By this time the Jodhpur Polo team was invincible and soon *jodhpurs* and were worn by all polo players within a very short time. Jodhpur also first popularised the *bundgala* or tunic coat that came later to be known as a prince's coat, a shorter version of the longer *sherwani* which was the court dress. The prince's coat came to be a familiar sight, complete with embroidery using gold threads, in 19th and 20th century Europe.

Phool Mahal in Mehrangarh is richly gilded and exquisite in detail. The intricate arches are enhanced by delicate scalloping and the royal colours, yellow and red, still dominate.

Sir Pratap: A Valiant Eccentric

A DELIGHTFUL ANECDOTE relates to Sir Pratap, Regent of Jodhpur, who combined the courage of the Rathores with the delightful eccentricities that came from befriending the British royals. Recalls his great-great-grandson of Sir Pratap's visit to attend Queen Victoria's golden jubilee on her formal invitation: 'Most of the rulers in those days used to stay at the Savoy, or in Claridges or one of the great hotels of London, but my great-great-grandfather when he arrived in England said he would stay at Buckingham Palace. Somebody politely told him that Her Majesty had not invited him to stay in Buckingham Palace, to which he replied, "Supposing I were to invite Her Majesty to Jodhpur, would I expect her to stay in somebody else's house or hotel? So, obviously, Her Majesty will not expect me to stay in somebody else's house or hotel." Upon which he forthwith entered Buckingham Palace.'

Born the third son of the ruler of Jodhpur in 1845, Sir Pratap often proved himself fearless. Even at the late age of seventy he accompanied his troops into the war trenches of France and Palestine. When they faced a very heavy offensive in Haifa and the troops of the Jodhpur Lancers fell back, he gave them very clear simple orders: 'You can go forward and be killed by the enemy's bullets, or you can fall back and be executed by me.' The Jodhpur Lancers took Haifa.

It is said of his loyalty to the Queen Empress and of his charge at Jodhpur that Sir Pratap himself coined the motto: 'A hundred good deeds cannot weigh equal to loyalty.'

There was always an oasis for desert dwellers to rejoice in; Jodhpur's is Gulab Sagar Lake, a small water body on the banks of which stand the Kunj Behari and Chamunda temples, shrines royale, housing the presiding deities of Jodhpur. These are located beside the erstwhile Raj Mahal.

Close to Mehrangarh, and of more recent vintage, is a memorial called Jaswant Thada. Built in 1899 using blinding white marble, it contrasts rather markedly with the basalt hill on which it stands, and is consecrated to the memory of Maharaja Jaswant Singh. One of its more interesting aspects is the complete genealogical table of the rulers of Jodhpur, and their portraits, which can easily be viewed here for a comprehensive grasp of Marwar's history.

Only a few kilometres from Mehrangarh is Mandore, the first Rathore stronghold and capital of Marwar. Little remains in Mandore today of that past—a few ruins and a more recent memorial. In all likelihood, the stone was pulled down from the buildings of the erstwhile capital and used in the construction of

These women belong to the Kalbeliya tribe. Kalbeliyas are gypsies from the desert near Jaisalmer who are known for their music, dance and snake charmer's skills.

Facing page:
A batter of rice flour is used to decorate the courtyards of even the most humble dwellings on festive occasions.

Mehrangarh, for raw material is not easy to get and carry in the desert. Mandore does, however, have an abundant number of cenotaphs, locally known as *chattris*, built to resemble temples. Umbrella-like canopies stand atop slim pillars, groups of them together. There is a separate group of such cenotaphs for the ranis. There is a Hall of Heroes here with life-size figures of legendary heroes, painted rather crudely and believed to be dedicated to three million gods; and the Ek Thambha Mahal, an old palace with delicate carvings, rising three storeys high. A small museum in the Janana Mahal contains some fine sculpture and miniature paintings.

Close by is Bal Samand, a lake and gardens with a 20th century palace that was a hunting lodge for members of the royal family. Built in 1159, the Bal Samand Lake is the oldest artificial lake in Rajasthan. Although the interior of the palace is European in style, it has entirely traditional red sandstone filigree windows and beautifully carved balconies.

Within the city is Ajit Bhawan, another palace hotel run by members of the ruling family who have crammed into this modest building almost all the memorabilia that came their way. While the original building has much charm and should be visited, also of interest are newly constructed cottages in the folksy tradition with local materials and interiors that are at variance with the grander, royal home.

Chamunda Devi, the fierce form of Durga, the mother-goddess, worshipped as Shakti by Rajputs; an idol at Mandore.

Left: *Jain idol from Jaisalmer: the Rajput rulers extended patronage to Jain traders who in turn built beautiful temples: some of the finest examples of stone sculpture are to be seen within the precincts of these temples.*

Along a Historic Route

North west of Jodhpur is the road that stretches like an artery connecting with Jaisalmer. Once the journey was done on horseback, for that is how the armies moved. The road for the most part is narrow, but traffic is limited and movement is swift. Camel carts trundle along this state highway, giving way to motorized traffic everytime the sound of a vehicle travels ahead. The camel and the cart are centuries old, the tyres on their wheels of the latest, most modern technology. Aeroplane tyres do two hundred landings before they are replaced. These tyres, at least in India, then find a very good market in Rajasthan where their size is ideal for camel carts.

When the hot winds, called the *luh*, blow in the summer, entire sand dunes are lifted and transplanted from one place to another. At such times, travel on the road sometimes becomes difficult. The best time to travel, therefore, is the winter, brief though it is. Even then it is advisable to carry one's own stock of water, aerated drinks and quantities of food. The journey will be punctuated with few stops, for there is little to view in the desert save its aridness and the stretching sea of golden sand.

The strategic importance of this area to the Indian Army means that the roads are very well maintained, so getting around is quite comfortable. The drive out of Jodhpur is a little slow, for the town is spread out, and several villages have now joined its suburban limits. The road will first direct you to Osian, off the highway. Surrounded by sand dunes, Osian has over a dozen Hindu and Jain temples said

Facing page:
The people of the desert are deeply religious; this priest from a temple keeps a watch on time, recounts legends and organizes religious ceremonies while counting the beads.

to have been built chiefly between the 8th and 12th centuries, Rajasthan's earliest group of temples. The earliest known temple is dedicated to the sun god, its carved pillars supporting a conical roof; within it is an image of Durga. The last of the great Osian temples, the Sachiya Mata Mandir is a living temple of the Golden Durga and was completed in the 12th century. The temple has a large assembly hall where devotees gather, and has images of gods and goddesses, apart from a profusely carved ceiling. Visitors now have the option of spending a night in the middle of the desert at the Camel Camp, situated on the highest sand dune. This is a complex of luxury tents with modern amenities.

Back on the road there are few diversions (from the route to Jaisalmer), which are well worth taking. The first is Khimsar, a desert castle, built by the fifth son of Jodhpur's founder, an important *thikana* under the state. Further along, a diversion off the main highway, is Nagaur, a fortified medieval settlement which became a centre of Chishti Sufis. Enter the town past a cluster of cenotaphs built in the Rajput style, looking like pristine stone-umbrellas. The town has a mosque ordered by Emperor Akbar when he visited Nagaur after a trip to the dargah at Ajmer, near Jaipur.

The vast Ahhichatragarh Fort, which houses palaces of the Mughals emperors and of the Marwars, is being restored with the aid of the Paul Getty Foundation. It houses wall paintings and ancient systems of rainwater conservation and storage. The restoration work carried out at the fort was awarded the 2000 UNESCO Heritage Award. Nagaur comes to life once every year when what is described as the world's largest camel trading fair takes place, usually in January-February, the date depending on the lunar calendar. This is a prosaic event with none of the colour and pageantry of Pushkar, but there is brisk trading. The men build campfires at night and sing ballads of unrequited love and of valour, and under the stars tranquillity settles on a scene that would not have been out of place in Biblical times.

Heading back on the road which leads to Jaisalmer lies the picturesque village of Khichan. The red sandstone havelis of the Oswal Jains are the main tourist attraction here while natural beauty

Stone tablets such as this, showing a man mounted on a horse and a woman alongside, usually mark sati-spots.

Facing page: *Watching life go by… . Such is the isolation of the desert that many of the modern conveniences are not even known here; when the rains come there are crops, though children can grow up and become men without having known a single rainfall.*

can be found in the way of sand dunes and a lake. The once quiet village is now a bustling agricultural center and a prominent bird-feeding station. Jain villagers put out grain for winter visitors and as a result up to 8,000 Demoiselle Cranes and occasionally Common Eastern Cranes can be seen in December and January on the feeding grounds.

The next stop is Pokharan, which is a popular mid-way stopover between Jodhpur and Jaisalmer for tourists as it was for royal and merchant caravans in the past. The 16th-century yellow sandstone Pokharan fort has a small museum with a collection of medieval weapons, furniture, costumes and paintings. Pokharan is also well known for its red and white pottery and terracotta figurines. Khetolai, about 25 kilometres from Pokharan is the site of India's two nuclear tests in 1974 and more recently in 1998.

Only 110 km from Pokharan lies the mystical town of Jaisalmer. First views fail to disappoint, as Jaisalmer rises from the heart of the Thar Desert like a golden mirage.

Desert life is harsh, and imposes climatic and social restrictions on people of the Thar. They carry water over long distances, cover their homes with thatch, and plaster them with a paste of cow dung, clay and pieces of hay, and then paint them to bring brightness to their otherwise bleak surroundings.

Facing page:
In their beautifully decorated, albeit simple homes, women carry on a conversation to make the weight of household chores seem lighter.

Jaisalmer

The lunar-descended Yadava family claims an important ancestor, Lord Krishna himself, forty-sixth in the line of descent, and Jaisalmer—the most western of desert kingdoms, considered till a few decades ago as inaccessible—is charmingly linked with him. Krishna played a crucial role in the *Mahabharata*, the epic battle between the five Pandava brothers whom he favoured and the hundred Kaurava brothers who, to a man, were killed. The mother of the Kauravas had cursed Krishna that upon his death, his sons for generations would be scattered and there would be no single place they would call their home. That came to pass, for soon after his death, the Yadava rulers were overthrown from their seat in Delhi and Dwarka. This did not end their power, however, for Yadava kings crossed the northwestern frontier of Hindustan to win themselves kingdoms in Afghanistan and beyond. Ghazni, in Afghanistan, was named after Gaz, twelfth in the line of descent after Krishna; driven out of there, the Yadavas established the city of Salihwanpur in what is now Pakistan. At this time, among the greatest of the warriors, Bhatti, conquered several lands for himself, and such was his might that the clan came to be known thereafter as the Bhattis; it is the Bhatti Rajputs who have ruled Jaisalmer.

Much before Jaisalmer, however, Mahmud of Ghazni wreaked terrible vengeance on the lunar-Rajputs, driving them to the fiery inferno of the Thar desert; the Bhattis settled here in the beginning of the 9th century. In the vast theatre of the desert they built a city, and with a trade route they could tax heavily, it became a city not

Facing page:
There is a close symbiosis between man and beast in the desert, both dependent on each other for survival in the harsh environment; it is common to find cattle, goats, sheep and camels wandering loose in villages, for ownership is respected.

Jaisalmer's fort, now referred to as Sonar Qila, was built in the 12th century; it has 99 bastions, and its rounded contours seem to ripple with the sand. The fort was the ruling base of the Bhatti Rajputs, who claim descent from the moon.

without riches. Isolated, with money at their command, they fought their fair share of battles, devoting the rest of their time to some of the most delicate stone architecture seen in the world. But back to Krishna and his association with Jaisalmer. It is believed that when Krishna and Arjuna, one of the five Pandava brothers, were passing through the Thar, Arjuna, feeling thirsty, requested Krishna for water. And Krishna with an arrow, or perhaps it was his divine discus, dug a hole in the earth near Trikuta hill, and there was sweet water for drinking. Years later, his descendants, driven to the desert, and having established their dynasty in this frontier outpost, circled the hill within an enormous wall 'with ninety-nine beetling bastions' and established Jaisalmer in the 12th century.

Jaisalmer was not the Bhatti's capital of choice. They raised their first fortification at Tanot, later at Deorawal, and finally took over the settlement of Lodurva. The rulers came to be called Rawals, and they controlled a city of considerable wealth, guarded by twelve gates. Complaints against the Bhatti stronghold reached Mohammmad Ghori, two of whose caravans had been raided by them. He sent in an army and had the city razed to the ground. Untold havoc was wreaked, and little of the city now survives but for a few temples.

Upon a hermit's advice, Rawal Jaisal laid the foundations for the fort of Jaisalmer in 1156. Raised upon an elevation, the fort is visible only from close by, so well does it blend with the sand that

The desert is peopled by a martial race, men proud of their past and unwilling to forgo it.

surrounds it. Also called the Golden Fort because of the colour of the sandstone, it dominates the town. Despite its age of seven centuries and three decades, the fort continues to be marvellously preserved, and is still inhabited, suggesting the manner in which fortified settlements were occupied under feudal monarchies. Recent commendable restoration efforts at the fort have ensured the protection of damaged buildings and awareness being created on the various threats to historical monuments in Jaisalmer. The Maharani's Palace, or Rani-ka Mahal, which was damaged in the 1993 monsoon today houses the new Jaisalmer Heritage Centre - an exciting project in itself, marrying contemporary museum design with traditional craftsmanship.

The Jain citizens who had settled in Jaisalmer raised the money for the first fortress wall; later, two more concentric walls were added made from the locally available yellow sandstone, blocks of which were used to raise the defenses complete with ramparts, turrets and towers. The rulers had by now risen in rank from Rawal to Maharawal, and Maharawal Garsi had the Garsisar water tank ordered, a substantial body of water that kept the settlement supplied. Within the fort there was an affirmation of faith of yet another kind. Temples were raised, both Jain and Hindu, with a surfeit of ornamentation in stone relief. As with all temples of the period, they attracted a great deal of wealth, and the idols tended to be spectacular. These are not all on display any more, but sometimes a temple priest may open the special cells wherein images are installed for a breathtaking view of some of the most expensive sculptures in the world.

The Bada Bagh was then laid as a garden on a tank with a drainage system designed uniquely to feed probably the only mango grove in the world. Overlooking Bada Bagh came up the final resting point of the Bhatti royals. Clusters of cenotaphs honour the dead, and tablets inscribed within each tell of valorous deaths, satis by ranis and by concubines.

Jaisalmer controlled a major outpost on the West Asian trade route and now offered sanctuary to artisans; its isolation increasingly kept it away from the battles that Jodhpur found

A Tale of Lovers

LIKE MOST LOVE STORIES of the desert, the tale of Moomal and Mahendra is a tragic one. Moomal was a princess from Jaisalmer who lived in the earlier capital of Lodurva. Many suitors approached the lovely princess, but she declined all of them. Prince Mahendra of Amarkot, who had heard of her great beauty, bribed one of her servants and sought out the secret entrance to her chambers, where he surprised her. The prince would journey every night from Amarkot, departing early in the morning. Strife between the two kingdoms made their legal union impossible.

On a visit home, Moomal's sister wished to see her sister's lover. Disguising herself as a minister, she waited in Moomal's chambers. Mahendra was late in coming that night, and the two sisters fell into slumber. When he did arrive, only to see his beloved apparently in the arms of another man, he left in a fury and never returned again. Moomal then disguised herself as a bangle-seller and set off for Amarkot, where she set up a game of chess with the prince.

During the game, Mahendra noticed on the bangle-seller's hand a mark similar to that of Moomal's. When he explained how his beloved had taken on a new paramour, she removed her turban, embraced him and told him the truth.

Sadly, the two lovers had suffered in separation, and both had developed a weak heart. In their embrace, both died, and now the lover's tale is celebrated in songs of the desert.

The royal palace located outside the fort, with its tiered Badal Mahal. Mounted atop the highest tier is the tazia *(metal ornament) gifted by the Muslim craftsmen who worked on the building.*

itself so frequently engaged in. When Jaisalmer started paying tribute to Delhi in the 17th century, peace was assured, and some of the finest buildings now came up. The trading community, with its considerable wealth, raised exquisite havelis that, though later copied by royal builders, could not be duplicated. The Maharawals created two more water tanks. Amar Sagar was built in the 18th century and grew into a temple complex. Mool Sagar was added in the early 19th century and as home of the Pushkarna Brahmin community, it featured its own wells, a palace and a small temple that is a duplicate of the original in the fort. In 1818, Jaisalmer became the last of the desert kingdoms to trade its autonomy for British protection, and this was the finest period in its history of haveli -building.

The first of these to come up were the Patwa havelis, five of them, known locally as Patwon ki Haveli. The Patwa family dealt in threads

of silver and gold to embroider dresses, but they made their money elsewhere, in the smuggling of opium and as moneylenders. With the proceeds of their substantial profits, the five brothers of this Jain family ordered five adjoining mansions for themselves. The major contribution in these havelis is that of unnamed, anonymous stone carvers, for every space on the surface has been utilized, carved profusely, delicate *jali* freizes keeping the interiors cool and offering privacy to the women who sat by them to look out without exposing themselves to the public eye. Built of the yellow sandstone that was used for the construction of most buildings in Rajasthan, the havelis, five storeys high, are honeycomb-like, with different designs on the surface of every window and arch. The architect and the sculptor obviously worked hand in hand to create the magnificent details which characterize them. The five havelis were raised in the period from 1800 to 1860. Two of these are now government property.

Garsisar, the water tank in Jaisalmer around which are built cenotaphs and temples. The arched entrance was built by Teelon, a courtesan.

The stone workmanship on Jaisalmer's havelis was influenced by Rajput architecture, amalgamated with the traditions of Islamic art that were imported via the traders' caravans through the desert. Many of these havelis are still occupied by descendants of their original builders.

The next haveli of some distinction to come up was what has come to be known as Nathmalji ki Haveli. Diwan Mohata Nathmal was the prime minister of Jaisalmer, and Maharawal Beri Sal had the haveli specially ordered for him. Interestingly, the ostentatious carving on the haveli was created by two Muslim brothers, Laloo and Hati. Each took on the onus of one side of the building, developed according to the same plan. But what a difference there was when these were completed, for the carvings were totally unlike each other, though in their quality these remain unparalleled. There were the usual geometric and floral motifs, but also carved into the walls were introductions of the then new age (such as trains and bicycles) that the carvers had never seen, but patterned out of hearsay. Completed in 1885, the building's entrance was flanked by two stone elephants to mark it as the residence of a senior state official.

Meanwhile, the Maharawal of Jaisalmer too felt the need for a more modern palace, and so the Silvataa community set about building him a confection of a palace. The earlier residence in the heart of the fortified town had not one but three palaces together, from a total of five of which one rose seven storeys high. The new palace, as it was built, had the by-now familiar *jali*-work of Jaisalmer's stone masons; the West Asian caravans that passed through Jaisalmer inspired much of its Islamic characteristics; there were Jain influences too; and mounted on top of the palace, as a gift from his Muslim masons, was a five-storey stone *tazia.* It was an imposing palace with a grand Durbar Hall, intricate filigree work on pillars and windows, and drooping Bangladhar roofs. But there is an element of severity in the palace, still the residence of erstwhile members of the ruling family; it is not in the same league as the havelis of the merchants.

The last among Jaisalmer's more distinctive havelis is again the 19th-century residence of the state prime minister, Salim Singh. His mansion rose eight storeys high when it was built, and was a grand structure; every surface was carved; he demanded and got the best. Work that did not please him was rejected, and new designs approved and incorporated. Of the 38 balconies the haveli boasts, each has a different design. The haveli began with a narrow base, and grew wider as it went higher. At the very top is a blue cupola supported on brackets carved in the form of peacocks.

Salim Singh's father, Diwan Swaroop Singh, a powerful, impressive prime minister, was murdered as a result of a court intrigue when Salim was only twelve years old. The son took it upon himself to avenge his father's death, and with such skill did he go about ridding Jaisalmer of its princes and courtiers that he was appointed Diwan by Maharawal Mool Raj as soon as he came of age. When Salim Singh built his haveli he occupied it

A beautifully sculptured elephant from a wall at Jaisalmer. The elephant is considered auspicious, and is also a symbol of royalty.

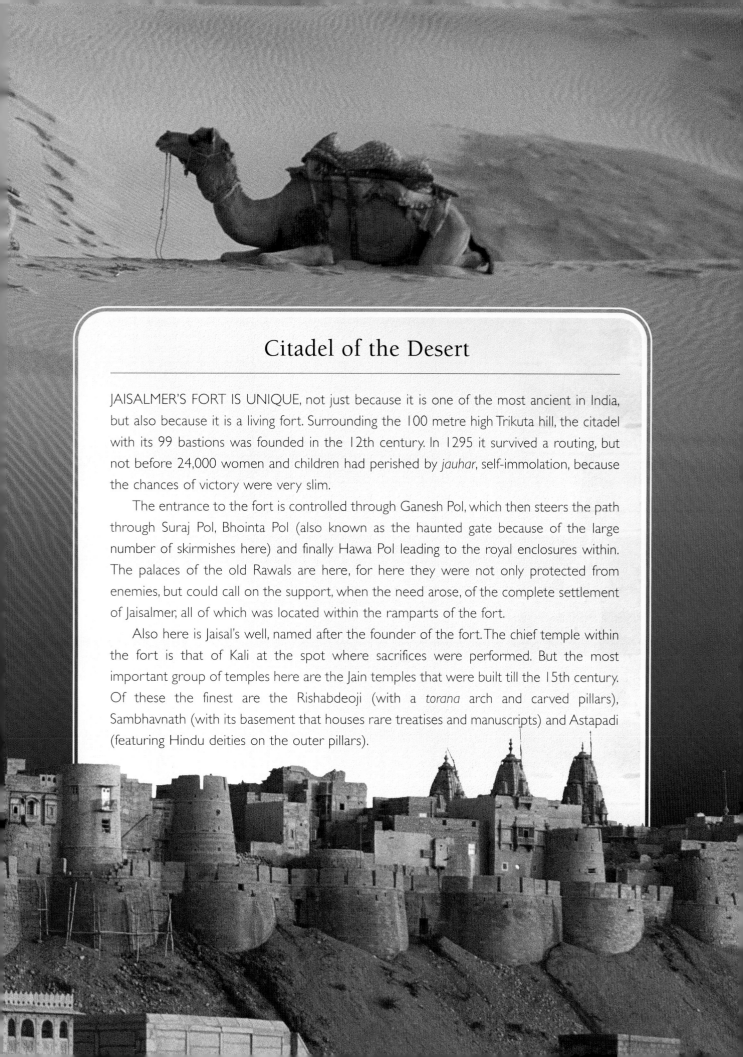

Citadel of the Desert

JAISALMER'S FORT IS UNIQUE, not just because it is one of the most ancient in India, but also because it is a living fort. Surrounding the 100 metre high Trikuta hill, the citadel with its 99 bastions was founded in the 12th century. In 1295 it survived a routing, but not before 24,000 women and children had perished by *jauhar*, self-immolation, because the chances of victory were very slim.

The entrance to the fort is controlled through Ganesh Pol, which then steers the path through Suraj Pol, Bhointa Pol (also known as the haunted gate because of the large number of skirmishes here) and finally Hawa Pol leading to the royal enclosures within. The palaces of the old Rawals are here, for here they were not only protected from enemies, but could call on the support, when the need arose, of the complete settlement of Jaisalmer, all of which was located within the ramparts of the fort.

Also here is Jaisal's well, named after the founder of the fort. The chief temple within the fort is that of Kali at the spot where sacrifices were performed. But the most important group of temples here are the Jain temples that were built till the 15th century. Of these the finest are the Rishabdeoji (with a *torana* arch and carved pillars), Sambhavnath (with its basement that houses rare treatises and manuscripts) and Astapadi (featuring Hindu deities on the outer pillars).

with seven wives and two concubines. He was checked by the Maharawal, however, when he proposed building a bridge from his haveli to the Maharawal's palace, and the two top storeys of his haveli were destroyed. Perhaps that marked a shift in his fortunes, for soon thereafter he was murdered in one of the very palace intrigues that he had so long fostered.

Garsisar, the main water tank and source of water supply to Jaisalmer, has a number of small shrines and temples built around its banks. It is reached through an interesting archway raised by a courtesan. Teelon, the courtesan, belonged to Jaisalmer though she was a court singer and dancer in Hyderabad (now in Pakistan). Once a year she would return to Jaisalmer, usually doing the short rainy spell, and distribute lavishly her wealth, ill-gotten though it was perceived to be. On one of these visits she had the archway erected as an entrance to Garsisar. When it was raised, courtiers

A view of the Jaisalmer fort from the rooftop of a nearby haveli. The fort is still a living entity today, and is inhabited by families who have been in residence for centuries.

Facing page:
Men gather at a window in the splendid Nathmalji Ki Haveli. Nathmalji was a Prime Minister at the palace and the haveli was ordered for him by the Maharawal of Jaisalmer.

The highest storey of Salim Singh Ki Haveli, residence of the scheming Diwan of Jaisalmer who got his just desserts when he planned to connect this portion of his house with the royal palace through an arched bridge.

expressed their concern that the king could not pass under a gateway raised by a prostitute. To keep his dignity intact, and yet not have the arch destroyed, Teelon had a statue of the God of Truth, Satyanarayan, placed atop it, and the court decree seeking the destruction of the arch was revoked.

Jaisalmer today is not so much a city to see as to experience. The fort, its people, their crafts, the havelis, a stay in the last of the royal residences to be built, Jawahar Niwas, and nearby excursions, call for no detailed itinerary. The ancient capital of Lodurva is close at hand. Little remains from the past, but there is still the *torana* archway of the entrance, and exquisitely carved Jain temples.

These temples are a hallmark in Jaisalmer. The Jain community controlled the business interests on trade routes and in turn was offered protection by the ruling families. The community built several temples beginning with Lodurva and continuing at Jaisalmer. Within the fort are a number of Jain temples, most dedicated to Rishabdeoji and Sambhavnathji, built in the 12th to 15th centuries, and richly represented

in carvings with mythical figures. There are also Jain temples at Amar Sagar, the water tank where a mango grove was raised, *en route* to Lodurva.

The decline of Jaisalmer set in with the beginning of the 20th century. No longer did major caravans pass through this route, for the British in India had established two major ports, those of Bombay and Calcutta. Local brigands raided the smaller caravans that passed through, as Jaisalmer could not offer them protection anymore. The citadel, which had grown on the money from the trade routes, ceased to be of importance. People moved out to seek their fortunes elsewhere, and at one stage the population came down to a perilous four thousand. Jaisalmer became lost to the world. People spoke of the wonders of a settlement that once was, believing it to be lost to them. And, far out in the desert, slumbering Jaisalmer did indeed seem like a town of the past, with

Within the Jaisalmer fort are a number of Jain temples; Jaisalmer's traders and money-lenders were of the Jain faith and gained the patronage of the Bhatti rulers.

little future. The Oscar-winning film director, the late Satyajit Ray, used the fort as the backdrop for one of his films, and the citadel came to be referred to thereafter as Sonar Qila, the Golden Fort!

Modern communications saved Jaisalmer. A road was built, and transport arrived, including the railway—today, the city also boasts an airfield. Tourism has revived its sagging fortunes. It is once again a city of activity, though it retains the wonderful, aloof air of a traditional Rajput stronghold. Fortunately, it will be many decades before Jaisalmer is part of the mainstream, and till such time there will always be its haunting beauty to captivate, a time-warp that is friendly and accessible.

In many ways Jaisalmer is a medieval town still, an isolated outpost in the desert, once so inaccessible that its population dwindled to a perilous four thousand.

Following pages 88-89: *These chattris near Jaisalmer are a scenic place for a quick stop.*

Around Jaisalmer

Amar Sagar, the once formal gardens and pleasure palace of Amar Singh on the bank of a lake continues to attract visitors today. A short ride (5 km) from Jaisalmer Amar Sagar also houses a recently restored Jain temple. A further 10 km away lies Lodurva which contains a number of Jain temples that are the only remains of a once flourishing Marwar capital. The temples are well maintained and worth a visit.

The charming ghost town of Khuldera is worth stopping at on the way to Sam. The town has an interesting story attached to it. Salim Singh, the then prime minister of Jaisalmer, took a liking to a local Paliwal girl from this village. However, her people did not want her to be taken away and so after intense pressure from Salim Singh they decided to abandon the village. Overnight the villagers left in different directions, never to return. It remains well preserved and has a number of interesting buildings.

The most pristine spot around Jaisalmer is undoubtedly where there are only sand dunes rising to a high crest, facing each other over short valley-troughs. Perhaps the most popular destination for sunset camel rides is the Sam dunes, 40 km west of Jaisalmer. It is not as remote as it once was yet the impressive views around Sam dunes are worth experiencing. Sit there on an evening when the sun is setting and listen to the ballad of Moomal and Mahendra, those legendary lovers, on the Jew's harp, or the *narh*, traditional musical instruments. If you come earlier, in the morning, this is the ideal place for a camel ride, or the launch of a camel safari into the yawning space of the desert as it swallows you up, and only your camel-driver to guide you back!

Spread around Jaisalmer, to its southwest, is The Thar Desert National Park, a vast biosphere reserve spread over 3,000 sq km for the protection and study of the fragile wildlife and eco-system, home to the endangered Great Indian Bustard. Desert reptiles, lizards, the Indian gazelle and chinkara, eagles and desert birds, including wintering species from distant Siberia, are also found here. And the inevitable, if scarce, *khejri* tree. Truly a fascinating birdwatching haven, The Thar Desert National Park is also home to blackbucks and desert cats.

Khuri, a small picturesque village, 40 km southwest of Jaisalmer, attracts visitors for its shifting sand dunes. The Sodha clan ruled this village of decorated thatched buildings for four centuries. An ideal detour to experience a peaceful sunset.

Some three hours drive out of Jaisalmer is Barmer, another desert town with little reason to be located in the midst of the sands.

The Jain temples are profusely carved, akin to the marble sculptures of the Jain temples at Ranakpur and the Dilwara complex near Mount Abu.

An aerial view of a typical desert hamlet. The walls of the huts are made of sand mixed with cow-dung, replastered regularly; the thorny scrub of the desert is used for fencing, and all around, for hundreds of miles, there is nothing but arid wasteland.

Again, it was trade routes that directed its foundation, and were responsible for its growth. Barmer never became as wealthy as Jaisalmer, its fortunes were always more limited. But, as at Jaisalmer, Barmer's artisans earned renown for a craft of great skill and patience, wood-carving; not the sculpture seen elsewhere, but the fine lattice-work of solid doors and windows, each little piece fitted in with tweezers, finely carved, but with a strength to the overall frame, and often inlaid. Distances and the journey into the desert did not allow it to grow out of Barmer, and it lay isolated here, so that very few people practise it now, and if their children take to alternate professions, the craft could well die out. It is also a major centre for wood carving, durrie rug weaving, embroidery and block

printing. The 10th and 11th century Kiradu temples, though badly damaged, are interesting. There are scattered havelis in Barmer, but many are now in ruins, eroded quite effectively by the sharp lacerations of sand.

The desert was once sea, as fossil ruins prove. It was also part of the belt where the Indus Valley Civilization flourished; this is evident from excavations of pottery at desert sites. Perhaps, some day, we will find the remains, not just of lost caravans, but of complete settlements—for kingdoms have flourished here. But in these desolate parts, the appearance and disappearance of such kingdoms would excite little comment. The desert holds its mysteries.

Following pages 94-95:
Jaisalmer's enchanting sunsets add greatly to its magical appeal.

Following page 96:
Men wear colourful turbans and jewellery: gold ear-studs are common and, on festive occasions, necklaces.